Michael Peckham

Look back at now
Paintings from Isolation

Cadmium Books

Published by Cadmium Books

Design: Rebecca Penmore

Coordinator: Maria Sin

Photography: Mel Allen

Printed in Wales by Gomer Press

ISBN 978-1-5272-9204-8

www.michaelpeckham.co.uk

Illustrations
Front cover: *Sentinel tree*, 2020, Monoprint, 24 x 19 cm
Page 4: *Peak sanctuary*, 2020, Monoprint, 18 x 14 cm
Page 10: *Plateau track*, 2020, Monoprint, 18 x 23 cm
Page 56: *The mad pomegranate tree 2*, 2020, Gouache on paper, 29 x 24 cm
Page 66: *Vaughan 1 All go into the light*, 2019, Acrylic on paper, 57 x 72 cm
Page 74: *Tree figure*, 2004, Oil on paper, 33 x 23 cm
Page 94: *Contadour 1*, 2018, Acrylic and ink on paper, 28 x 40 cm

Dimensions of all works of art are given height before width.

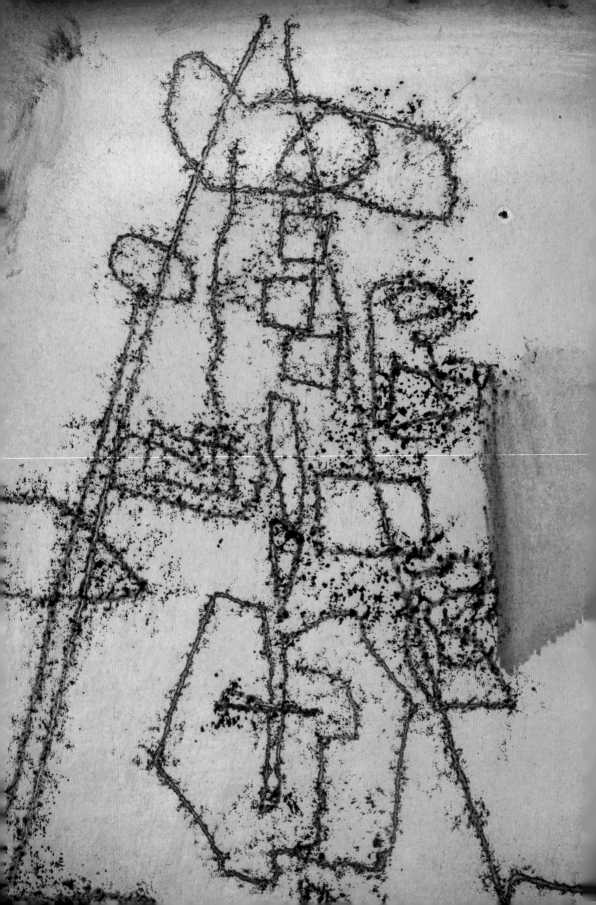

" *The only thing I would like to be able to teach is a way of looking, in other words a way of being in the world.* "

Italo Calvino

" The treasures of time lie high, in urns, coins, and monuments, scarce below the roots of some vegetables."

Sir Thomas Browne

Most of the paintings in this book were made in 2020 during the Covid-19 pandemic, over several months of lockdown on a patch of land on a steep hillside that leads to an Iron Age fort. The place, an island in forty-five acres of field, abuts on a landscape shaped by the Neolithic, Roman, Medieval, and more recent past. Viewed from afar, the track from the plot resembles the wake of a passing boat, its edges churned by the wind that ripples in waves across the vegetation. Isolation, with the connotation of *isola* —island—more accurately describes the state of being confined to this remote parcel than the brutal term lockdown. The months spent in isolation here stimulated thoughts about separation and interconnectedness in relation to the many and varied islands visited in the past: Easter Island with its astonishing display of massive figures (*moai*) carved from volcanic rock looking out over the Pacific Ocean thousands of kilometres from the nearest landmass; Akdamar a small island with a tenth-century Armenian cathedral set in the brilliant blue-green alkaline waters of Lake Van in Eastern Anatolia. Or, cancer workshops in the 1980's on the small island of San Servolo in the Venice Laguna, an island that had once been the site of a Benedictine monastery, convent, and mental asylum—islands, you might say, within an island. Paradoxically, then, thinking about islands—or thinking with islands—became a means of generative association; of bridging different places and times with the now of pandemic isolation.

> "[Massimo] Cacciari's original idea was to conceive of the 'opera' as an archipelago made up of many islands. Therefore no scenes but islands, so that the so-called path of the 'opera' would be configured like a wandering navigation among these islands."

Luigi Nono on *Prometeo* (1987)

At around the time of the workshops on San Servolo in the 1980's, the Venetian composer Luigi Nono was completing his major work, the opera *Prometeo*, on the nearby island of Giudecca. Nono, who only had a few years to live (he died in 1990), was forging a novel approach to music seeking to extend its range and to embed it in the broader context of theatre and politics, as well as the new technologies that were becoming available to produce and manipulate sound. *Prometeo* doesn't only draw on Nono's long interest in the Prometheus myth, but also on his study of early ecclesiastical music. The first performance was given in the disused church of San Lorenzo on Giudecca in 1984, with the performers placed in a large wooden structure designed by the architect Renzo Piano to resemble a violin, so the sound would resonate inside and outside the structure. A model of Piano's creation can be seen together with an archive of Nono's scores and other memorabilia in his foundation on Giudecca. *Prometeo* is an island piece in every sense, with sections of the composition explicitly designated as *isola*. Nono commented on the different tonalities and pitches of the church bells that reached his island asynchronously across the Laguna day and night. He saw them not only as calls to work and meditation, but also as warnings. The overall effect of listening to *Prometeo* is of meditative ceremony and rare poetry. It isn't difficult to grasp the spatial and auditory features of *Prometeo* in the charged aura of the hill-fort landscape. The music contributed to the context in which these paintings were made during the months of isolation.

Live island, 2002
Acrylic on paper, 50 x 72 cm

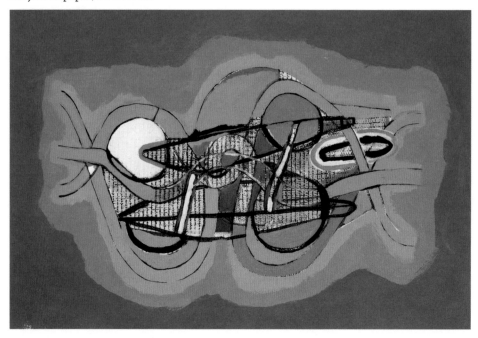

Nono's notion of archipelago and interconnectedness resonates with novel ideas in the quite different field of quantum physics. Italian physicist Carlo Rovelli recounts the story of 23-year-old Werner Heisenberg who in 1925 spent the summer on the rocky island of Helgoland in the North Sea to relieve his hay fever and reflect on atomic structure. There, he conceived of a radically different view of the interior of the atom and laid the basis for quantum theory described by Rovelli as the theory of how things influence each other: objects do not exist in isolation, they continuously interact with each other. The world is a dense web of interactions. "The quantum world is more tenuous than the one imagined by the old physics," he observes; "it is made up of happenings, discontinuous events, without permanence. It is a world with a fine texture, intricate and fragile as Venetian lace. Every interaction is an event, and it is these light and ephemeral events that weave reality, not the heavy objects charged with absolute properties that our philosophy posited in support of these events."

Isolation on a remote island in the North Sea yielded insights that not only revolutionized physics and led to a vast array of new technologies, but also promoted a re-evaluation of our assumptions about the nature of 'reality,' setting the very concept of island and isolation in a new light.

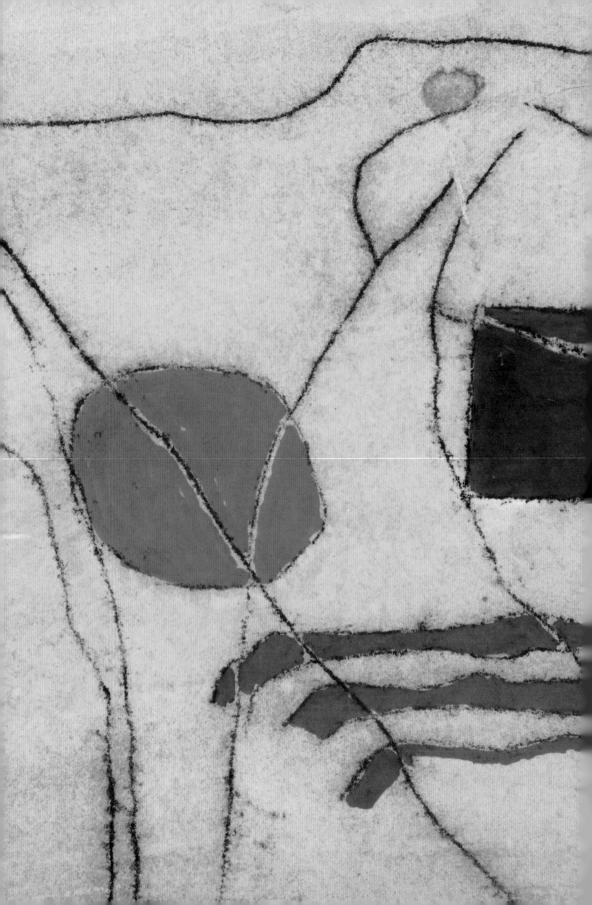

Deep track

The fort above the island in the fields—an impressive earthwork with two banks around the perimeter each with a ditch—occupies the top of the hill. It is flanked by woods and looks out over a narrow valley on the slopes of which the boundaries of field systems ("Celtic" fields) dating from the Bronze Age are visible when the sun casts an oblique light. Even when they are not, the eye searches instinctively for the potential symmetry of an almost visible protuberance. It's as if the land is a body that needs to be read for some telling mass. This is a place of mysterious shapes; a landscape sculpted by humans over millennia. It is shaped by stone circles, henges, barrows, burial chambers, mounds, dykes, clay pits, flint mines, dew ponds, and field enclosures. In the hill fort, moles and rabbits occasionally turn out shards of pottery among fragments of flint and clay. Even today, despite centuries of erosion, segments of dyke between brambles are impressive in their depth.

When you spend time here you begin to appreciate human tenacity and the persistence of ingenuity, not only in the earthworks, but also in the objects—decorative and votive, as well as utilitarian—that come to the surface. Creating hill forts, dykes, and barrows was a massive undertaking. It required digging out and repositioning vast quantities of earth with tools that may seem primitive today but were themselves the products of honed skills and inventiveness.

The landscape is traversed by tracks: Roman causeways, Anglo-Saxon *herepaths*, drovers' roads that follow ancient ridgeways, and a network of public footpaths. Separated

by a deep narrow valley the fort looks over to a causeway,
once a Roman road. The land is bathed in sound: the
mewing of red kites, the forlorn cries of sheep, deer
barking at night, the grating sound of a tractor striking
flint, helicopters and jets flying overhead from military
bases on Salisbury Plain. The wind is the backdrop and
super-generator in this varied soundscape that ranges
from the barely audible to the thunderous; from the
full-tilt blast of a storm to the dry leaves that rattle "like
tin over the asphalt." The trees in the woods around the
hill fort have a quality of madness, too. Their trunks are
gaunt, frivolous, and anthropomorphic. The boughs of
a large beech tree are carved with dates and initials so
high and perilously placed that one wonders how a steady
hand could reach them. Stretched by years of growth,
these arborglyphs have overgrown their borders, merging
message with medium. The human urge to be remembered
is forgotten now in the compact flesh of tree.

Magic hill, 2020
Oil on canvas, 100 x 70 cm

Blue field system, 2020
Gouache and ink on paper, 33 x 28 cm

Red track, 2020
Ink and gouache on paper, 32 x 21 cm

Hill figures, 2020
Acrylic and pumice, 87 x 83 cm

Celtic fields 1, 2020
Acrylic on canvas, 100 x 70 cm

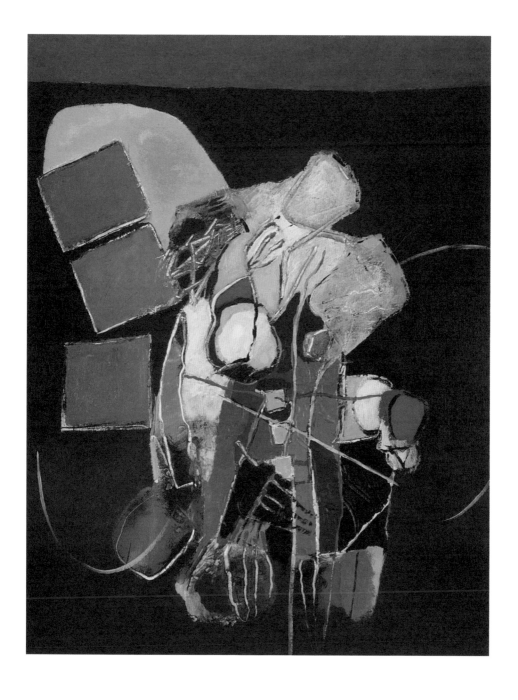

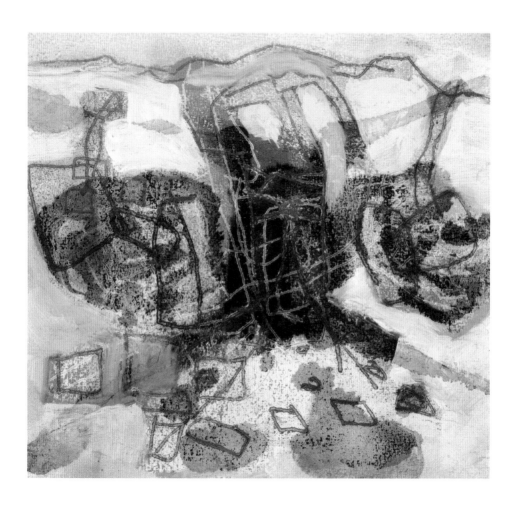

Sunrise, 1976/2020
Built out collage, 84 x 59 cm

Storm, 2020
Acrylic on paper, 27 x 29 cm

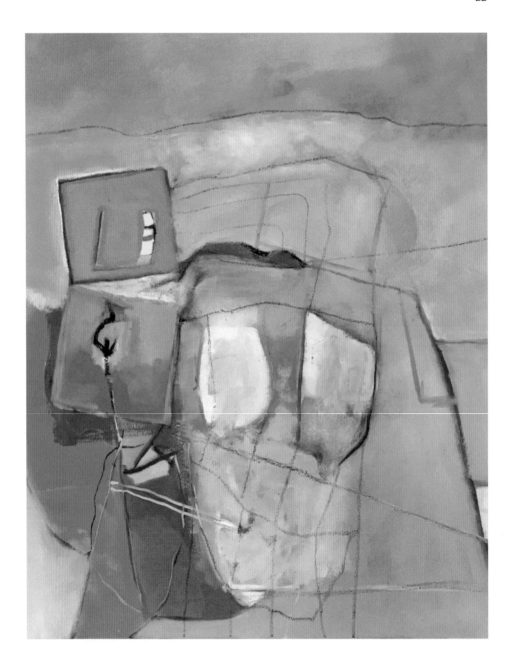

Celtic fields 2, 2020
Oil on canvas, 100 x 70 cm

Enclosure, 2020
Acrylic on paper, 21 x 28 cm

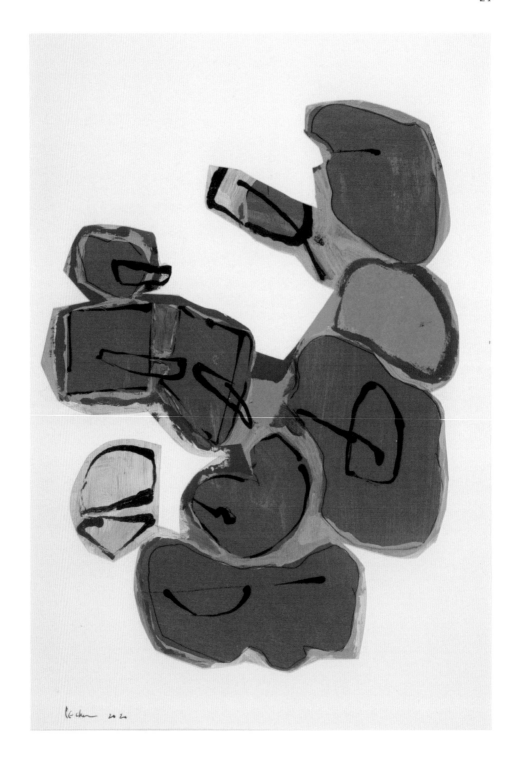

Out crop, 2020
Collage, 33 x 22 cm

Field circuitry, 2020
Acrylic on paper, 26 x 18 cm

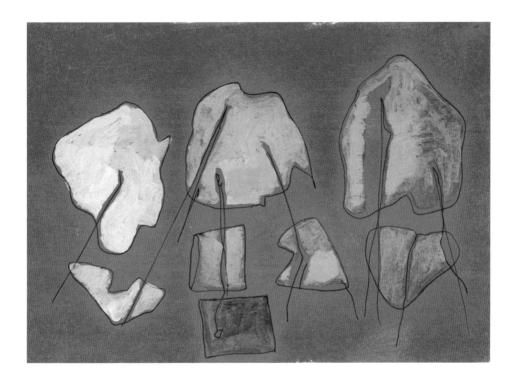

Red aisle, 2020
Acrylic on paper, 30 x 19 cm

Leafwrap, 2020
Acrylic on paper, 24 x 18 cm

Hillfort complex 1, 2020
Gouache and ink on paper, 23 x 30 cm

Lunar track, 2020
Acrylic on paper, 26 x 20.5 cm

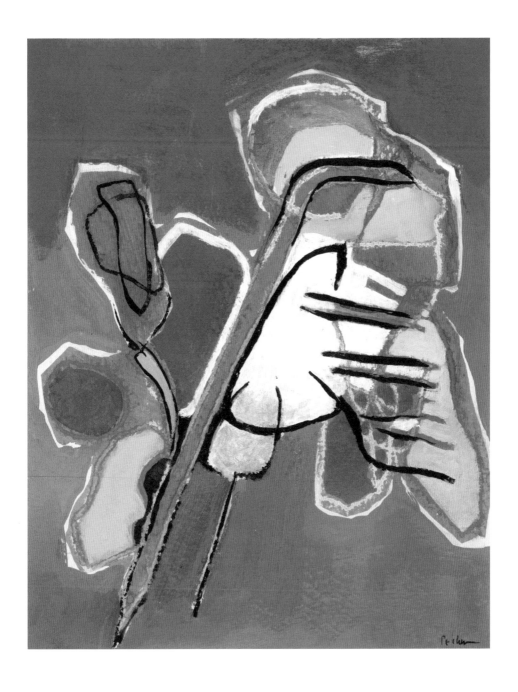

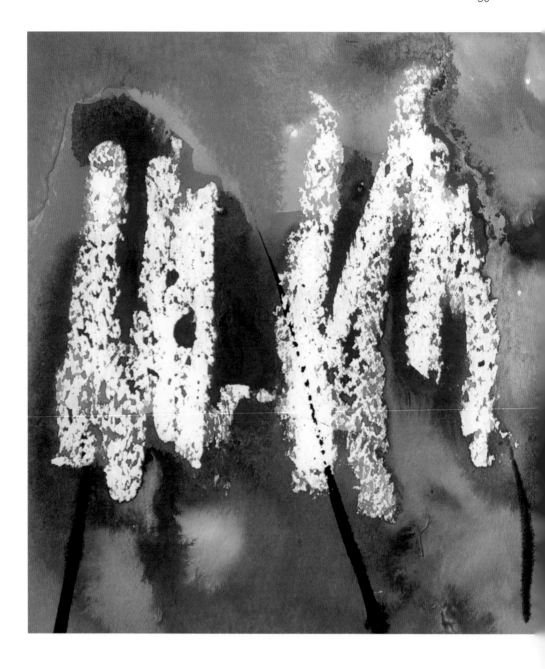

Tree fringe 2, 2020
Watercolour and wax on paper, 12 x 23 cm

Tree fringe 1, 2020
Watercolour and wax on paper, 19 x 28 cm

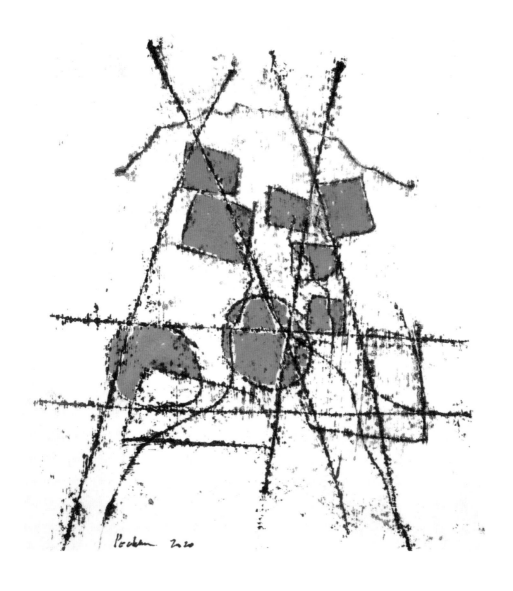

At the peak, 2020
Monoprint, 20 x 18 cm

Blue woodside, 2020
Gouache on paper, 12 x 17.5 cm

Fort script, 2020
Watercolour and wax, 20 x 29 cm

Overleaf:
Hillfort complex 2, 2020
Gouache on paper, 29 x 37 cm

The mono-prints were made with etching ink and khadi paper. The paper was coloured with oil paint and white spirit applied with a sponge. The drawings transferred from glass were mainly of simple forms in spaces evoking hill, track, trees and fort. In mono-printing, lines are transformed into nervous and edgy tracks with an aura like that of the trajectory of subatomic particles in a cloud chamber.

Sentinel tree, 2020
Monoprint, 24 x 19 cm

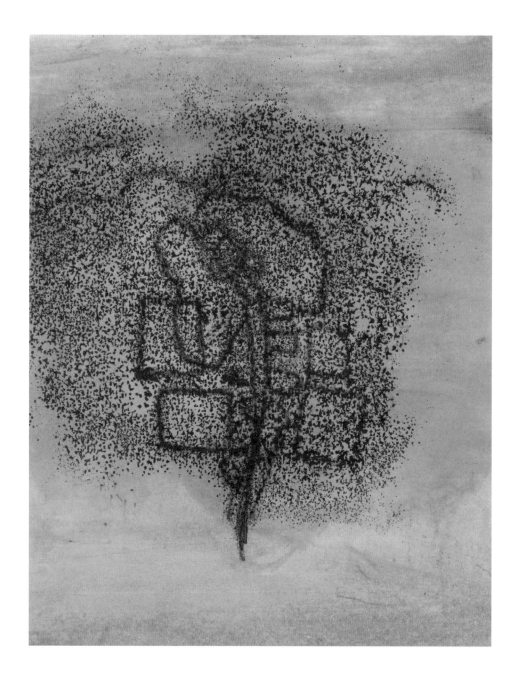

Sanctuary tree, 2020
Oil on paper, 37 x 27 cm

Deep track 1, 2020
Monoprint, 25 x 21 cm

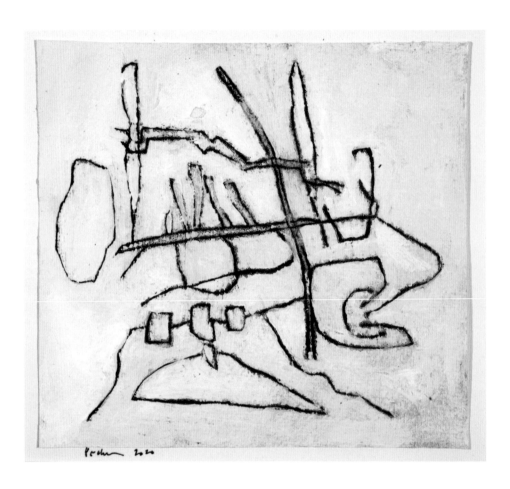

Deep track 2, 2020
Monoprint, 17 x 18 cm

Peak sanctuary, 2020
Monoprint, 18 x 14 cm

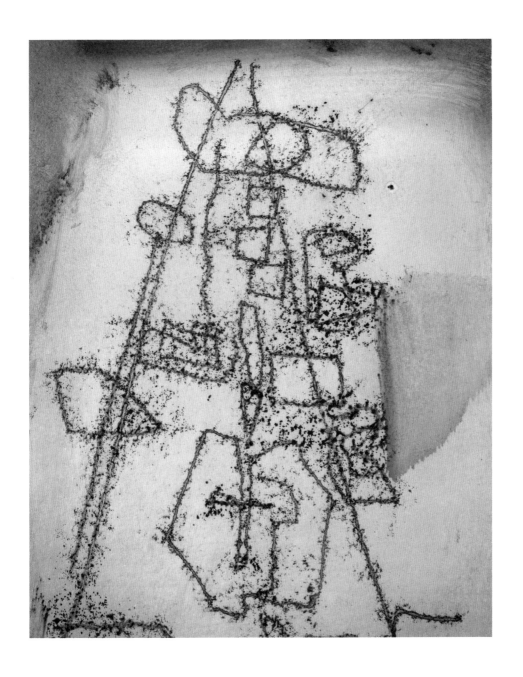

Inscribed hill 1, 2020
Monoprint, 19 x 19 cm

Content of track, 2020
Monoprint, 20 x 13 cm

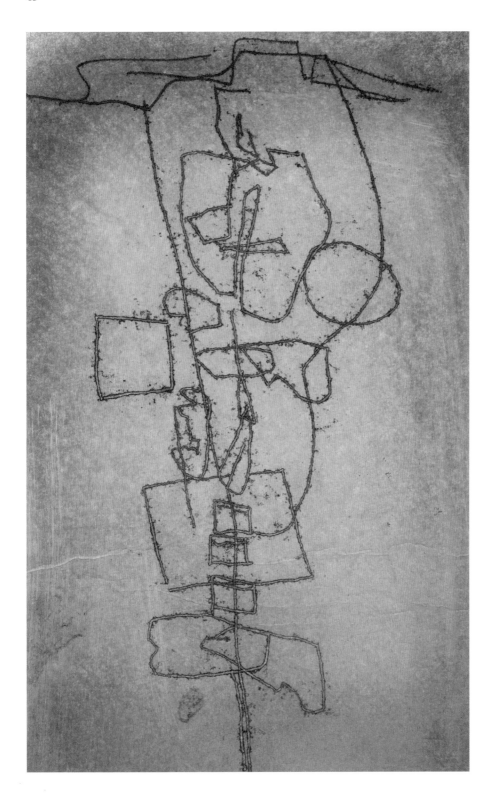

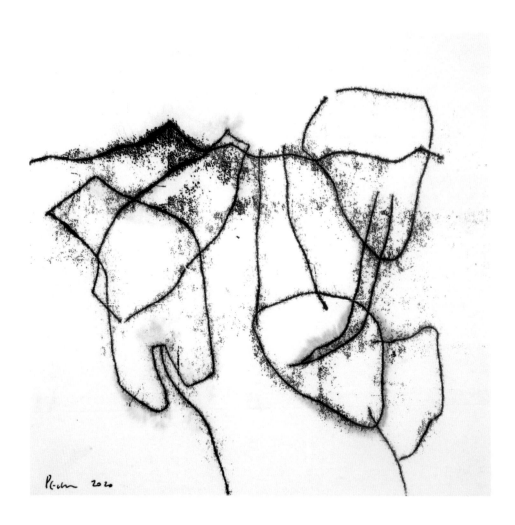

Inscribed hill 2, 2020
Monoprint, 18 x 18 cm

Bronze hill, 2020
Monoprint, 17 x 21 cm

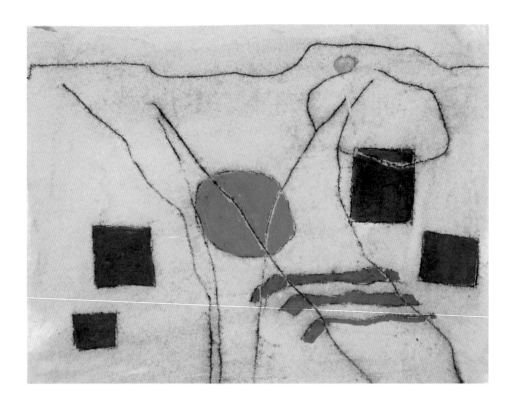

Plateau track, 2020
Monoprint, 18 x 23 cm

Fort topography, 2020
Monoprint, 21 x 27 cm

Hill fragments, 2020
Monoprint, 17 x 17 cm

Deep track 4, 2020
Monoprint, 20.5 x 18 cm

Hill rise, 2020
Monoprint and pencil, 17 x 15cm

Deep track 7, 2020
Monoprint, 20 x 14 cm

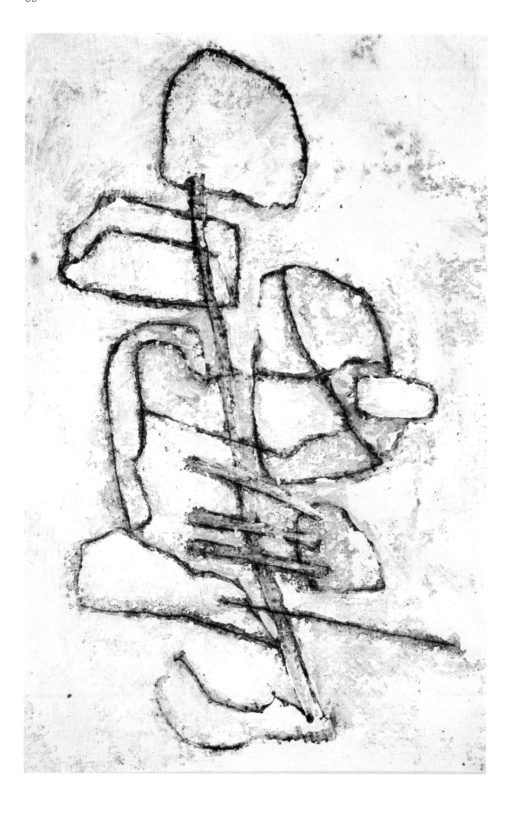

Earth clatter, 2020
Monoprint, 24 x 25 cm

Golden way, 2020
Monoprint, 17 x 10 cm

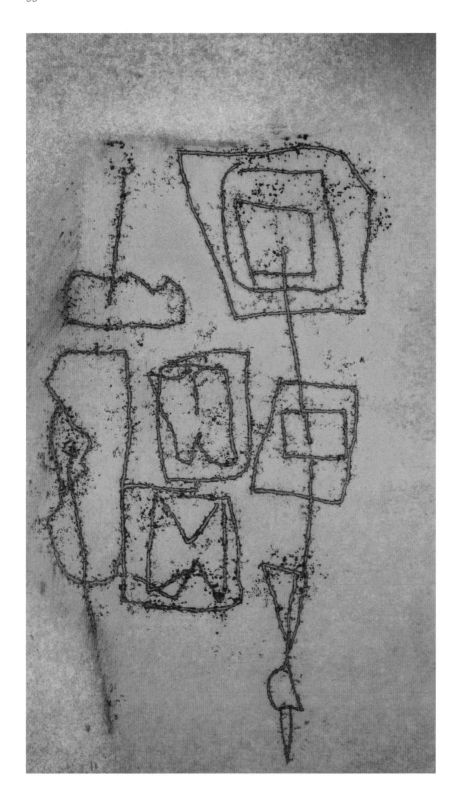

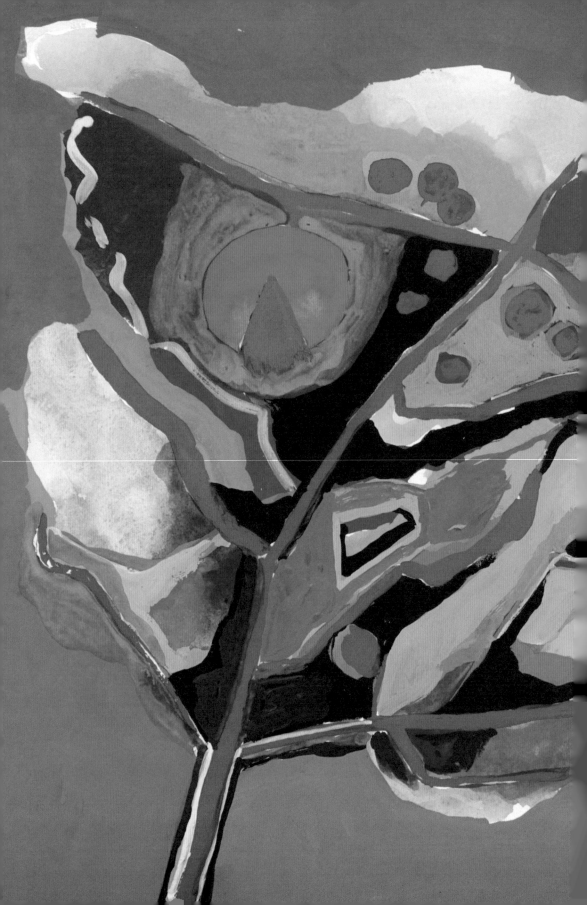

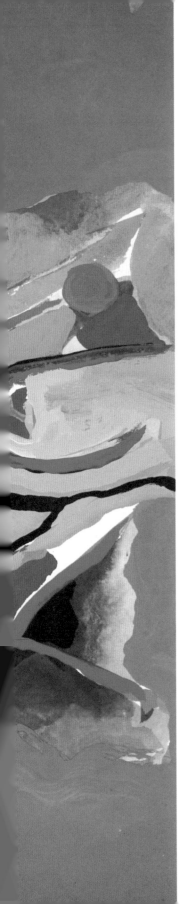

The Mad
Pomegranate Tree

" *For all art speaks through analogy.*
A line, straight or curved, a sound,
sharp or low-pitched, translates a certain
optical or acoustic contact. We all write
good or bad poems to the extent that
we live or reason according to the good
or bad meaning of the term."

Odysseus Elytis

The poetry of Odysseus Elytis is charged with strong
visual imagery. The four paintings included here
derive from his poem 'The Mad Pomegranate Tree'.
A celebration of vigour and colour, the tree is a beneficent
presence bringing light and life to a troubled world. As
Elytis himself once remarked, "I write so that black does
not have the last word." And yet there are hints of shadow,
too, in the unnerving wind that 'maddens' the tree—like
those trees that flank the hill fort—and in the allusion to
"the cloudy skies of the world" that are locked in perpetual
'combat' with the light:

On plains where the naked girls awake
When they harvest clover with their light brown arms
Roaming round the border of their dreams – tell me,
Is it the mad pomegranate tree,
Unsuspecting, that puts the lights in their verdant baskets
That floods their names with the singing of birds – tell me,
Is it the mad pomegranate tree that combats the cloudy
*   skies of the world?*

The pomegranate has an ancient heritage as a symbol of fertility and rebirth (it may have been the forbidden fruit in the Garden of Eden). But it also has darker associations. In Greek mythology, the goddess Persephone whose name evokes natural abundance, was abducted by Hades, god of the underworld. The promise of being released back into the world of the living was forfeited when she was tricked into eating pomegranate seeds. This condemned her to spend six months of each year in the underworld during which time the earth was barren. In the summer and autumn, when Persephone re-entered the upper world, the earth was once again fruitful.

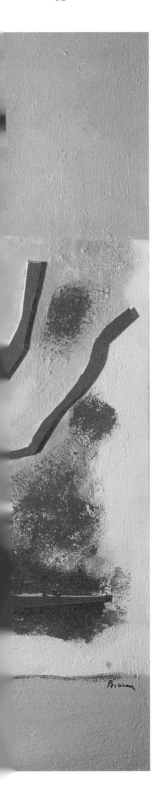

The mad pomegranate tree 1, 2020
Acrylic and foam board on canvas,
102 x 102 cm

The mad pomegranate tree 2, 2020
Gouache on paper, 29 x 24 cm

The mad pomegranate tree 3, 2020
Gouache on paper, 40 x 30 cm

The mad pomegranate tree 4, 2020
Acrylic on paper, 41 x 28 cm

Vaughan Trilogy

" *There is at all times (though shut up) in you*
   A powerful, rare dew,
   Which only grief and love extract…"

Henry Vaughan

Three paintings are based on themes from the work of the seventeenth-century Welsh poet and physician Henry Vaughan whose family home was Tretower Court in the Usk Valley near the Brecon Beacons. Vaughan, a devout Christian, lived most of his life there, drawing for his imagery on the spectacular landscape around him. Neglected for more than a century after his death, there was a revival of interest in his poetry in the twentieth century. In Vaughan's verse intense spiritual meditation is enriched with close observation of the natural world around him.

Two of the three Henry Vaughan paintings explore the notion of hidden life in quiescent nature: of the seed growing unseen, of an incipient awakening.

The third painting derives from the poem "They Are All Gone into the World of Light." Vaughan has climbed the hill behind his house and as the sun goes down, he reflects on the mystery of death and the purpose of life. Conjuring the image of an empty nest, he wonders where the bird has gone and "what fair well or grove he sings in now/that is to him unknown."

Vaughan 1 All go into the light, 2019
Acrylic on paper, 57 x 72 cm

Vaughan 2 The hidden greeness, 2019
Acrylic on paper, 57 x 72 cm

Overleaf:
Vaughan 3 The hidden greeness, 2019
Acrylic on paper, 57 x 72 cm

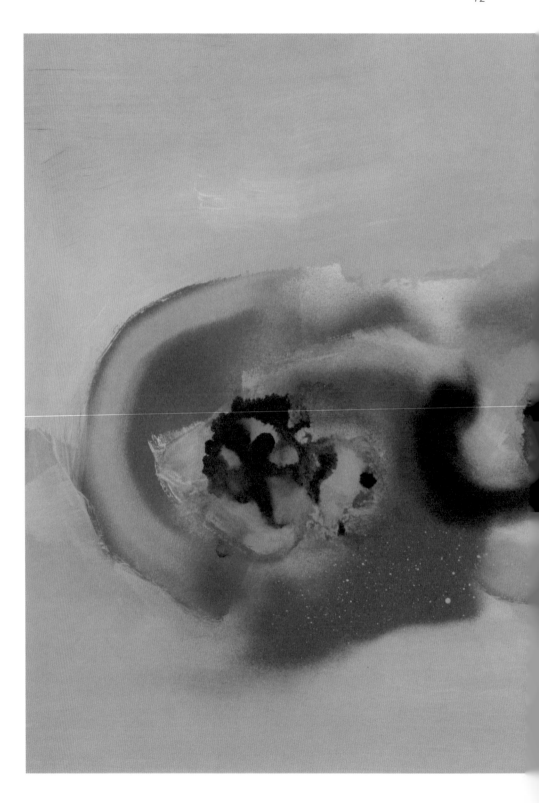

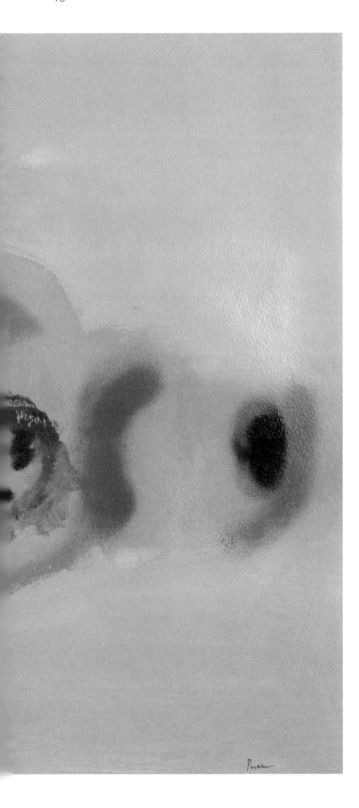

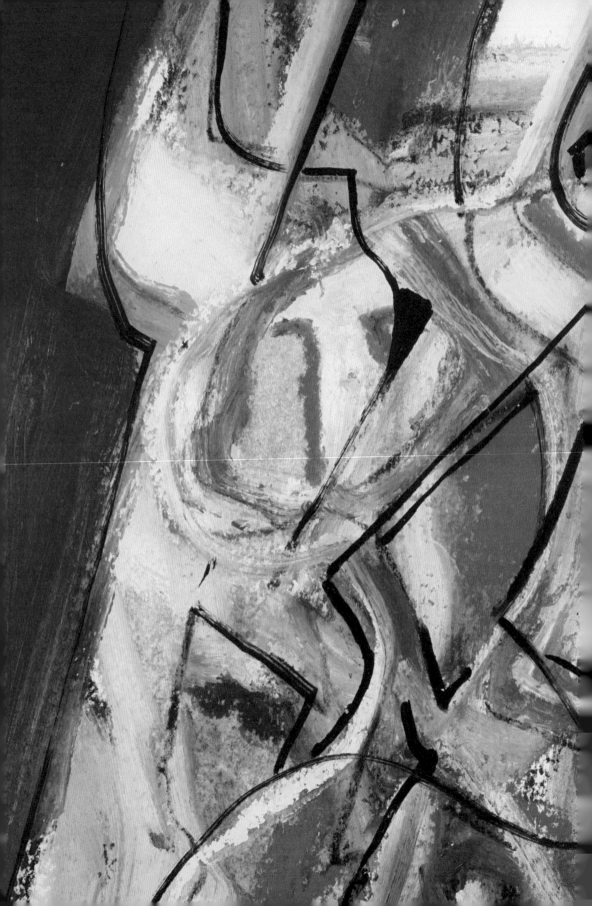

Hill Figures

The hill-fort island in Wiltshire was first encountered in the early 1990's. The trees fringing the plot were fresh and vigorously alive in the wind and there was a sense of intrusion entering the precinct at the main entry point to the east past a dew pond which might well have been there when the fort was in active use. The immense arena had a particular atmosphere. The branches and foliage evoked figures in motion and forms that conflated body and tree. Massive trees that had toppled in the Great Storm of 1987 enhanced the sense of unknown events. The association between humans and trees, of course, recurs in legend. In Welsh mythology the beautiful Blodeuwedd was created from the flowers of broom, oak, and meadowsweet for magician and warrior Lleu Llaw Gyffes who was forbidden to marry an earthly woman. Among the stories of transformation that Ovid tells is that of Daphne who while pursued by Apollo turns into a laurel tree.

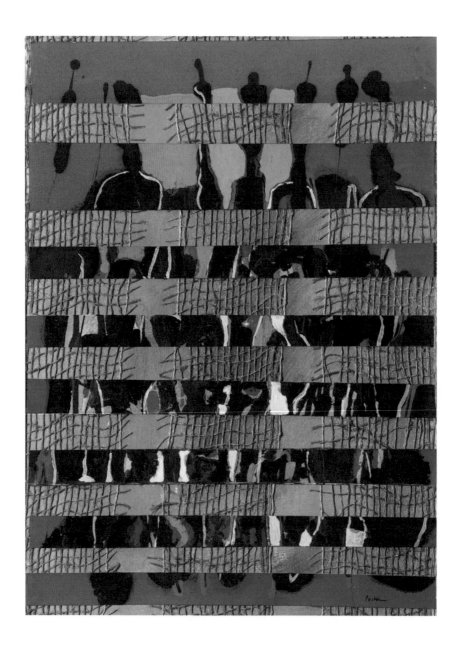

Gathering, 2019
Acrylic with scrim on paper, 42 x 31 cm

Tree figure, 2004
Oil on paper, 33 x 23 cm

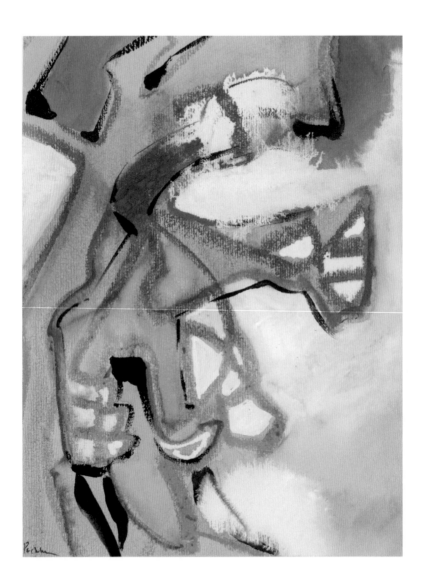

Forest figure 7, 1996
Watercolour crayon, 20.5 x 15 cm

Plinth man, 1996
Gouache on paper, 36 x 27 cm

Overleaf:
Dynamic figure, 1995
Gouache, 19 x 25.5 cm

Red coat in the wind, 1994
Gouache, 30.5 x 23 cm

Overleaf:
Forest figure 3, 1995
Pastel and guache, 26 x 16 cm

Forest figure 10, 1996
Acrylic, 13.5 x 8.5 cm

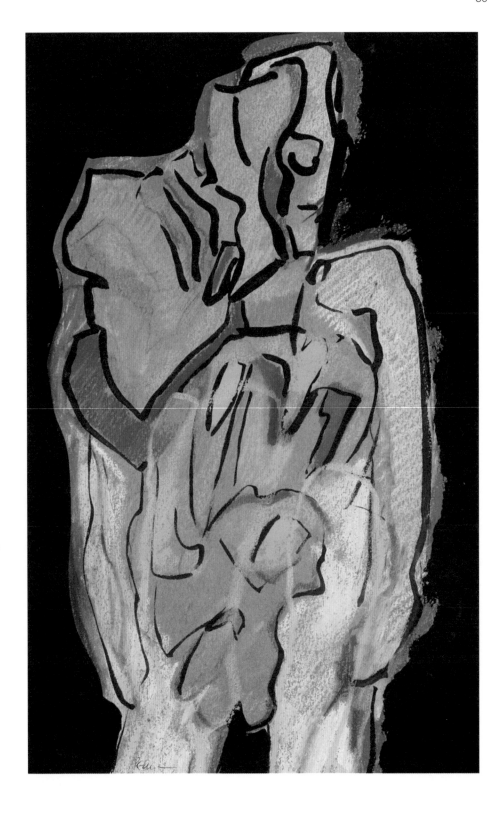

Forest figure 8, 1996
Gouache, 17.5 x 14 cm

Forest figure 4, 1995
Gouache on paper, 30 x 22 cm

Tree sanctuary, 1997
Oil on canvas, 122 x 152 cm

Blue flower 1, 1999
Collage, 28 x 32 cm

Blue flower 2, 1999
Collage, 27 x 29 cm

Outer Earth

" All man's errors arise because he imagines that he walks upon an inert thing when really his footsteps press themselves upon a flesh full of life."

Jean Giono

If the topographical features of the earth move us, they can also induce fear. We're fearful and curious of what lies beneath. Paul Cézanne was preoccupied by the under-earth that shapes the landscape, and he lamented that he wasn't a geologist able to delve below the surface of Mont Sainte-Victoire. Le Contadour in the Alpes-de-Haute-Provence provided the context for some of the paintings in this section. The rocky plateau is a remote place formerly inhabited by shepherds whose dry stonewall dwellings are still in evidence. The terrain is open to the sky and buffeted by winds from the nearby Montagne de Lure. There is a vivid sense in this landscape of a human pre-history. The writer Jean Giono had a strong attachment to this part of Provence. He believed that earth energy currents came near the surface in certain outcrops; at these locations gods and spirits interacted with humans. Paul Nash talked of the spirit of place in relation to his landscape paintings. The distinctive atmosphere of a particular place might be thought of a series of signals about its nature and history that emanate from the ground. Encountering the stone monoliths at Avebury and associating their presence and meaning with the spiral growth of convolvulus, Nash talked of solving "such an equation" in his art, as though the emissions of these disparate entities might be detected and transcribed. The naturalist W. H. Hudson who wrote about the life of a shepherd on the Wiltshire Downs, describes "the barrows, lynchetts and other mysterious mounds" as "chance hieroglyphs scored by men on the surface of the hills."

Helen Chadwick said of her large panels 'Viral Landscapes' in which images of the Pembrokeshire coast are overlaid with cells (from her own cervix), that the impulse for the work was a stimulus to know something that doesn't have form, yet is an emotive or physical force.

On walks over the downs you might come across a field dotted with treasure hunters prospecting the ploughed earth with their metal detectors. There is a congruency between Nono's compositions and the signs discharged from the earth as material relics and sounds, from jets breaking the sound barrier to wind vibrating through the wing feathers of a wood pigeon in flight. *Isola*, as Nono recognized, is the place where the past reconnects with the present, art becomes life, and the empty nest is re-occupied, at least here, for now.

Contadour 1, 2018
Acrylic and ink on paper, 28 x 40 cm

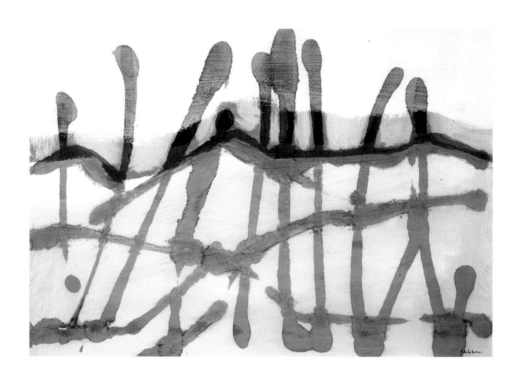

Contadour 2, 2018
Acrylic and ink on paper, 28 x 40 cm

Overleaf:
Reflected sky, 2018
Cutaway collage, 33.5 x 53 cm

Hot wind, 2018
Cutaway collage, 29 x 44 cm

Shoal, 2018
Cutaway collage, 14 x 20 cm

Billowing wind, 2018
Collage and acrylic, 30 x 39 cm

Sky spaces, 2018
Collage, 30.5 x 41 cm

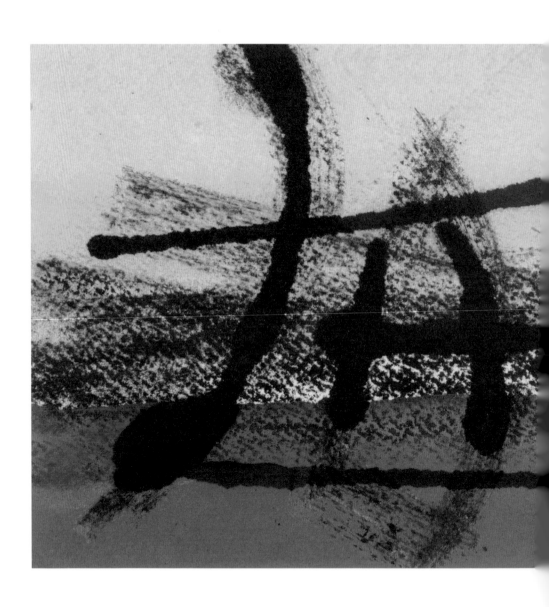

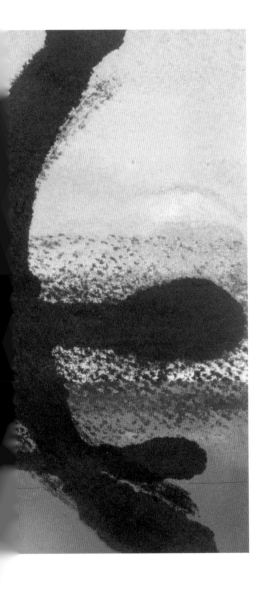

Plateau script, 2018
Gouache and ink on paper, 12 x 19 cm

Figure text, 2018
Gouache on paper, 14 x 22 cm

Flight script, 2018
Acrylic and ink on paper, 13 x 19.5 cm

Dance, 2017
Ink on paper, 13 x 19 cm

Plateua drawings, 2018
Gouache and ink on paper, 19 x 25 cm

Signals, 2018
Acrylic and collage on paper, 28 x 40 cm

Hill sounds, 2018
Acrylic on paper, 18 x 22 cm

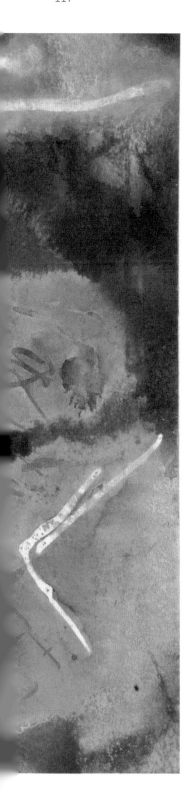

Palimpsest 2, 2010
Gouache on paper, 20 x 21 cm

Palimpsest 1, 2010
Gouache on paper, 20 x 21 cm

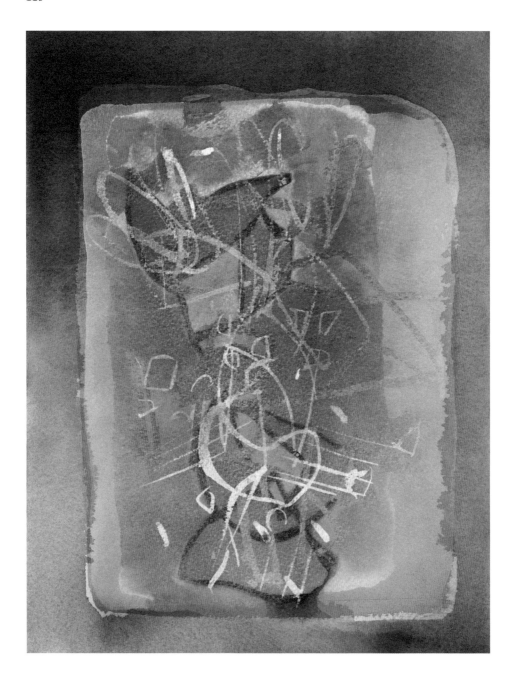

Overleaf:
White language, 2018
Acrylic ink, 30.5 x 40.5 cm

Palimpsest 3, 2010
Gouache on paper, 30.5 x 23 cm

Flow signs, 2017
Gouache and collage, 20 x 36 cm

Rock letters, 2018
Ink and scrim on paper, 23 x 30 cm

Biographical Note

From his early years Michael Peckham has embraced both art and science and had his first solo exhibition soon after he qualified as a doctor. A profile in *The New Scientist* in 1991 commented, "there are not many senior medical researchers in Britain who would list the political upheavals in Paris in 1968 among their formative experiences. There are fewer who read Czech poetry, or have their paintings exhibited regularly in London and Edinburgh." An essay, "One Life" commissioned in 2017 by *The Lancet* described the mutual influence of art and oncology in his work.

Michael Peckham was born in Wales and educated at William Jones West Monmouthshire Grammar School, St Catharine's College Cambridge and University College Hospital Medical School, London. He was called up for National Service in 1960 and spent two years as medical officer to the 2nd East Anglian Brigade. He left for Paris in 1965 where he worked on leukaemia at the Gustave Roussy Institute. In 1973 he was appointed professor at the Royal Marsden Hospital and Institute of Cancer Research. One of his contributions in medicine has been in the treatment of testicular cancer and Hodgkin's Disease where dramatic advances were made in the 1970's and 1980's. He was knighted in 1995. He and his wife Catherine were married in Paris as students and have three sons.

The works shown in Peckham's first solo exhibition at the Bear Lane Gallery in Oxford in 1964 were oil paintings predominantly on the theme of landscape. He had previously exhibited in mixed shows at University College North Wales (1962) and Somerville College Oxford (1963).

His first solo exhibition in London was at the Woodstock Gallery in 1970. The work marked a departure from landscape with an emphasis on a circle motif and built-out three-dimensional collages. The latter theme was developed in subsequent exhibitions at the Upper Street Gallery, Islington (1976) and the Consort Gallery (1982).

He first exhibited at the Christopher Hull Gallery in 1983 and over the next twenty years Hull became his agent. The 1983 show included thirty-six watercolours and in 1989 he exhibited sixty works ranging from large oil paintings to smaller works in gouache, crayon, ink and oil pastel. Two further exhibitions with Christopher Hull followed in 1992 and 1997.

In an exhibition at the Richard Demarco Gallery in Edinburgh in 1989 he gave a talk on "Salvagism" recounting his experience of retrieving rejected materials and making use of fragments of time. He worked with Demarco on the project "Death, Life, Regeneration," held at an international cancer congress at the South Bank in London in 1989 featuring work by Helen Chadwick, Joseph Beuys and Paul Neagu.

By the late 1990's Peckham's work drew more explicitly on his experience in science and medicine. Fifty paintings

Sand island, Crete, 1983, Gouache, 49 x 28.5 cm

and collages were exhibited under the title "Bodyworks" at the Millinery Works Gallery, London, in 2001. A selection of figure paintings using scrim, netting and hessian was shown at the Institute of Child Health Gallery in 2004. Later that year thirty-five drawings made in the clinical notes of patients under his care were shown at the Royal Academy Summer Exhibition under the title "Treatments."

In an exhibition in Tryon Street in 2013 he drew on the mythic story of Philomena and metamorphosis. In 2017 at the Millinery Works Gallery he explored the tension between visible surface and concealed depth in relation to the human body in an exhibition entitled "Balance of the Interior."

In 2020, a book of his paintings and collages (1963 – 2018) was published under the title *Balance of the Interior*. A book-launch planned for March 2020 at the East London Headquarters of Cancer Research UK (CRUK) had to be abandoned because of the Covid-19 pandemic. Three of Peckham's large canvases are exhibited in the atrium.

Readings

Sir Thomas Browne, physician and polymath, was the author of *Religio Medici* (1643) and *Hydriotaphia, Urn Burial, or, a Discourse of the Sepulchral Urns Lately Found in Norfolk* (1658), an essay stimulated by the discovery of the Walsingham cremation urns. There, Browne reflects on the likely origins of the buried artefacts.

The Italian novelist and short-story writer Italo Calvino was a masterful letter writer. The quote is taken from a letter to the editor François Wahl included in *Italo Calvino: Letters, 1941- 1985* (Penguin, 2014).

The phrase "like tin over the asphalt" comes from 'Little Gidding,' the final poem of T. S. Eliot's *The Four Quartets* (1942).

'The Mad Pomegranate Tree' by the Greek poet Odysseus Elytis was included in his first collection *Orientations* (1939). The excerpt quoted here, translated into English by Edmund Keeley and Philip Sherrard, is from the anthology *Six Poets of Modern Greece* (Thames and Hudson, 1960). Elytis's lyric poem reflects his interest in surrealist writing, and is also a counter-blast of light amidst the gathering clouds of war. Katrina Anghelaki-Rooke quoted Elytis's admission "I write so that black does not have the last word" in her obituary of the poet published in *The Independent* (March 22, 1996).

On the artist Paul Nash's engagement with the Neolithic

landscape of Avebury, see his "Contribution to Unit One," in *Paul Nash: Writings on Art*, edited by Andrew Causey (Oxford University Press, 2000), 107-110.

A Shepherd's Life: Impressions of the South Wiltshire Downs (Methuen & Co. Ltd., 1910) by the writer and naturalist W. H. Hudson tells the story of those, like the shepherd Caleb Bawcombe, who labour on the land, struggling to survive. The book is also an elegiac evocation of a fast-disappearing rural world.

Born in Manosque, Jean Giono's novels are set in Haute-Provence and celebrate nature and the life of rural communities there. Giono later produced films. *Cresus* (1960), a comedy, is set in the forbidding landscape of the Contadour.

Luigi Nono's selected writings and interviews have been published as *Nostalgia for the Future* (University of California Press, 2018). The collection includes an autobiographical essay, chapters on musical analysis and composition, music and theatre, and portraits and dedications.

Carlo Rovelli's book *Helgoland* (Allen Lane, 2021) tells the story of the physicist Werner Heisenberg who laid the basis for quantum mechanics on a remote island in the North Sea.

Henry Vaughan, physician and poet, was born in Tretower in the Usk Valley near the Black Mountains and Brecon Beacons and spent his life there. Although Vaughan was aware of Welsh bardic traditions, he wrote in English and was closely associated with the metaphysical poet George Herbert.